Born to Thrive

A Practical Guide to Creating Success

Kamaria Heru

Copyright © 2017 Kamaria Heru

All rights reserved, including the right of reproduction in whole or part in any form.

ISBN-10: 0692832351
ISBN-13: 978-0692832356

Dedication

I dedicate this work to every person who has that deep feeling that he or she is meant for more. You are not alone. I hope to inspire you to find the courage to give your inner excellence a chance to thrive.

Disclaimer

This book is written as a source of information only. Any advice or ideas presented do not supersede the advice of a physician, health advisor, or any other professional. Neither the author nor this book is responsible for the actual attainment of success or claims that the achievement of each attribute will guarantee successful outcomes. The author and publisher disclaim any responsibility for any damages or adverse experiences as a result of the information provided.

The ideas and stories presented in this book are solely a reflection of the author's interpretation of events derived from interviews and other media outlets. The author does not personally know or hold any affiliation with the artists and celebrities discussed. No harm or damage is intended to any party mentioned. Some details of events, names, and dialogue have been modified or omitted.

Contents

	Prologue	i
1	The Definition	1
2	The Requirements	4
3	The Attributes	23
4	The Conditions	55
5	The Calling	59
	Epilogue	65

Prologue

The quality of a person's life is in direct proportion to their commitment to excellence, regardless of their chosen field of endeavor.
—Vince Lombardi

If I know anything about humanity, I know that most of us aspire to a better way of life. Culturally, Americans are raised to chase the American dream, and immigrants long to thrive in the land of opportunity. But with all that fantasizing, few people seem to actually live the dream of getting to that better place in life. Why is that? With all the gurus promising you this and the experts guaranteeing you that, why do so few of us get to thrive? The answer seems simple to me: thriving is a choice. But I wondered, if choosing is the obstacle, then why do so few people choose prosperity? Isn't that what we all want?

I think it is human nature to want more, but it takes effort to actually get more in life, and therein lies the rub, as they say. After observing so many of my peers, both older and younger, I've noticed that most of us are so bogged down with trying to achieve basic survival that it is hard to direct our energy toward what it takes to thrive, let alone to make efforts toward doing so. How many people do you know who worry about money incessantly? They spend most of their time trying to keep their heads above water, cycling through debt habits that keep them anxious and angry about life. This is not the behavior or mentality of someone who can thrive.

I suspect that there is a little bit more than choice involved in what allows people to thrive. Choice is definitely the foundation of change, but I have found other qualities that support prosperity as well. When studying those I admire, I noticed common themes in their stories. There were certain choices, traits, and perceptions that seemed to allow them to step off the hamster wheel of survival and thrive.

Like Carl Rogers, a humanistic psychologist known for his work on self-actualization, I believe that every person can achieve his or her goals, wishes, and desires. Rogers argues that there are specific conditions that make "growth" (or self-actualization) more attainable (McLeod 2007). What I find more interesting is how few people who are raised under these conditions fail to develop certain characteristics that produce prosperity. Does that mean that we are destined to struggle if we didn't start off under the right conditions? I don't believe so, which is why I add to his argument by acknowledging that choice plays a role in pursuing this endeavor.

Let me clarify what I mean when I say *want*. We all want something. I don't know anyone who is short on aspirations or desires. Instead, I am referring to desiring something enough to endure what it takes to have it. Notice I used the word *endure*. That was not an accident. The pursuit of prosperity can be a tiresome marathon, testing your faith and patience every mile.

What I find fascinating is how often we sit back and admire others, particularly celebrities, and their ability to achieve excellence, as though it is something beyond our own potential to grasp. We say to ourselves, "What makes them different?" We feel connected to them, yet they sit on a pedestal as though what they do is just beyond our reach. We see ourselves in them, yet somehow they've found a way beyond the point where we are limited.

I find it human nature to want to compare our journey to someone else's; however, this has proven to be unwise. The reality of it is these people are not necessarily in possession of something we don't have but rather willing to do something that we have not yet surrendered to doing. Think of it like this: you have chosen to survive your life instead of living it. You have chosen that safe, cushy job rather than pursuing your passion. You have chosen the road heavily traveled instead of following your heart. You are making these choices to feel safe. It is much safer to dream than to do.

This is nothing to feel shame about. We all do it. Survival is a basic human instinct, and creating stability is a part of that. The problem lies in our becoming comfortable with complacency, failing to evolve further and actualize our potential. Once our survival needs are met, what is stopping us from going a little further? Fear. I am confident that most of us are suffering from some mental and emotional limitations. Most of my clients are not without talent or intelligence; instead, they are deeply afraid, wounded, and without guidance.

I will discuss the paralyzing power of fear in an upcoming chapter, but for now, at least understand that the perfect preparation and most optimal opportunity don't exist. And if they did, how would you even know there wasn't a bigger boat coming along in five minutes? You wouldn't, and so you'd be waiting for another five minutes and another five minutes until all the boats had gone, or worse, you'd drowned. You can't mess up an opportunity that is for you. I've seen many people bounce back from their mistakes, myself included. If you believe you are destined for greatness, then that is precisely what you will eventually produce. My encouragement in this book is to help you understand what it takes to jump off the intimidating cliff of possibilities. I make no promises that it will be easy but instead offer you the comfort of knowing that your struggles and insecurities are quite normal. You are never alone.

Why is thriving so important? Maybe you are satisfied with having a degree and a well-paying job and working until retirement. That is exactly what you were taught to do, and it is what makes you happy. Isn't that the point of all this: to be happy? Yes, but my encouragement here is for you to live to your fullest potential. When you choose to honor your potential, you contribute to the evolution of humanity. When you suppress your gifts, you are not honoring the excellence built within your soul, and often times, that breeds unhappiness.

I do not believe that for the centuries that human beings have been roaming the earth, we were simply meant to survive generation after generation. With each generation, we have the opportunity to do better and be better, and that starts with you. You were born for a reason, and you need to deeply understand and accept that. With that comes the responsibility of pushing beyond your personal limitations and the limiting paradigms of thought. This is where the real work comes in. This is where it is not enough to be chosen. We must choose.

If you are thinking to yourself, "But you don't understand what I've been through. You don't know where I come from. Every time I try, I get hurt." And so on and so on. I do understand, and you are shouldering the burden of every dreamer. The pain is real, and the path is not easy, but all we need is for it to be possible. I don't say this lightheartedly; you must be willing to go beyond your fears and walk into the darkness of the unknown in order to see who you can really become.

If you are that person who sits at your desk surfing the web because you are unfulfilled, who goes to concerts daydreaming about being onstage, or who watches television pretending it's you giving that acceptance speech, then you know the burn of your potential. That fire burning inside you is your potential calling you to be great. To live in excellence unapologetically. Despite what you may have heard, dreams are not just for people who want to get hurt. They are for people who want to excel, innovate, and push the human race forward to the level of greatness that we can achieve. We are all excellent in our own ways.

If you are feeling afraid, then you are normal. If you don't know what to do, then you are like me and every other person who had to start somewhere. The truth is that with all the information available to us and all those who have gone before us, there is no certain path to walk into our excellence. Everyone is different and requires a different mental, emotional, and spiritual evolution in order to get to the same place. This is how it begins. Acknowledge that you don't have all the answers, but you are willing to try. You don't know exactly what to do, but you know what you want, and you are willing to work. I invite you to choose excellence over complacency. I invite you to consider being calculatedly unsafe instead of fearful. I invite you to explore that thought or feeling that says you can do better because chances are you really can.

Chapter 1
The Definition

It had long since come to my attention that people of accomplishment rarely sat back and let things happen to them. They went out and happened to things.

—Leonardo da Vinci

For many years, I held the same definition of success as many others, which was based on the tangible and narrowly defined products of our society. As a young person entering the corporate world, I chased the possibility of a high title with six-figure pay, hoping that my work ethic and sacrifice would get me to the top. After nearly ten years of watching my peers get promoted over me, being tactically blocked from advancement opportunities, and enduring the microaggressive and sometimes racist abrasions of my work environments, I finally surrendered to the idea that my definition of success had to change. I had been confronted with the glass ceiling so many times that I had to release the idea that *that* was the only way to be successful.

The truth is success can be defined in many ways. For a long time, being able to have enough money to travel the world, buy my own house, drive the car of my choice, and take as many Pilates classes as I wanted were my definitions of what a successful life would look like. When I couldn't achieve that vision no matter where I worked or how much I sacrificed, I had to redefine how I saw myself and my life to learn what was driving that vision. In essence, that was my idea of achievement and the source of inner peace. If I didn't have to worry about money and could do anything I wanted with my time, then that was success for me. I thought having the title and pay would bring me that, so I chased it.

From this, I learned that success is much more broad and intangible than I was making it out to be. Because my self-worth was tied to my ability to attain these achievements, I found myself in a vortex of unhappiness, unaware of the cause and unable to resolve it. I was seeking validation from my oppressors and trying to achieve success in a system that was designed for me to fail. I couldn't understand what I needed to do to change the outcome. Naturally, I was forced to self-reflect since the external variables were not going to change. When I evaluated what was frustrating me, I found that it was not just the difficulty of the process of creating success and how indeterminable actually achieving it can be, but the nonstop-ness of the effort required to achieve it. That nugget of enlightenment broke open a different understanding of what problem I was really trying to solve: ease in my life.

My pursuit of success always had the narrative of greatness to it in order to characterize its intense quality. However, achieving greatness is possible without the lights, camera, and action. It does not have to contain the overwhelming intensified effort and difficulty of its depiction. The energy is a lot less antagonistic. Yes, struggle can breed greatness because it forces you to dig deeper inside yourself to overcome the obstacle. But for everyday folks like myself, most of us can achieve it through the effort we give to the work that we do every day. And honestly, that's all these professional athletes and celebrities are doing anyway. To demonstrate excellence in anything, you have to be willing to give the best of yourself to it. Whether you want to make sure every spot on that floor is mopped clean or every department of your company is functioning to its highest potential, you must give your best efforts. Now, I will be careful not to undermine the struggle embedded within the process of giving your best effort to what you do. Any expression of excellence within an environment committed to mediocrity will render conflict and provoke antagonists. We'll discuss more of this later.

So, the look of success had to change for me. It didn't include a red carpet with interviews. It no longer needed a crazy travel schedule to promote my books and seminars. It was more simply defined as being available to do my work in service of excellence. I needed to write my book, self-publish it, and begin to share my message. My goal still had responsibility in it but with less pressure to "be" something, thus, creating the ease I was looking for. There were no more timelines or deadlines. My future prosperity wasn't riding on it anymore. It was a simplified understanding of what it means to be successful.

Now, this may not be the definition that everyone comes to, but I illustrate my journey to help you find a piece of yourself within it. Becoming successful is naturally an antagonistic process. Nobody is great or successful by accident. It requires constant and concerted effort. Whether the goal is happiness, tangible products, or specific achievements, the acquisition process is the same. To understand a little more about this process, let's review the requirements.

Chapter 2
The Requirements

Endurance

All through my life, I have been tested. My will has been tested, my courage has been tested, my strength has been tested. Now my patience and endurance are being tested.

—Muhammad Ali

Glory is not given to the weak. The aspiration of success is often glorified and fantasized about, but the true path is not for the faint of heart or the impatient. You must endure the lessons. You must endure the expansiveness of time. This was one of the last lessons I learned about success. When you are young, the concept of time is hard to understand. It is hard to respect it as a real factor in the equation of creating a result. Whether it's due to short attention spans, our instant gratification culture, or a weakened ability to move through adversities, time is a difficult entity to comprehend, especially for our generation.

I would like to create an awareness of why time must be appreciated. In short, we have to develop a deeper, unwavering sense of self. To misunderstand who you are is to leave yourself vulnerable to manipulation. You better be damn straight that people will try to manipulate you. We have to move through each of our lessons fully and completely. To take shortcuts or skip a beat along the path leaves us vulnerable to careless, and perhaps costly, mistakes that compromise our progress. You better be damn certain that whatever lesson you don't learn will reoccur until you do. In essence, there is a maturity, certainty, and clarity that you want to acquire so that whatever success you attain is sustainable. Success requires readiness to receive it. This readiness can only be developed over time. Those who achieve success too quickly tend to fumble if not fold in the wake of it. I, obviously, don't want that for either of us.

I'll be honest here and say that I have a real issue with patience. I wait for no one. I tend to move fastest on my own. I've worked for companies that promised promotions and leaders that said they would look out for me only to test how committed I was to my own self-worth. After six months, I'd find out there was never a position created or they had already given the role to someone else less qualified. I'd abruptly leave the company and take my talents elsewhere. After a few years of that, I realized it was becoming a pattern I had to solve. I don't take kindly to disrespect and I have even less tolerance for bullshit. Welcome to the workforce.

Now, let's consider the concept of endurance. There are obstacles, adversities, and antagonists along everyone's path. They take different shapes, forms, and frequencies, depending on how steep the learning curve needs to be. Whether you are battling internal demons or external gremlins, the struggle is real. I learned late in the game that it is not about eliminating these grievances from your path but learning to effectively deal with them and move along your path in spite of them. This goes back to knowing yourself and your strengths and vulnerabilities, as well as your triggers and anchors. Perspective on yourself and others will prove to be your golden ticket out of the minefield. Once you understand the tactics people like to use to provoke you and who typically makes it habit to push your buttons, it is a lot easier to control.

Kim Kardashian, a reality television personality, has

had her share of adversities to endure. It couldn't have been easy building a beauty empire from a sex tape, but she managed to withstand the criticism, ridicule, and ostracism that came with her path. This is not to promote or condone her choices and behavior; however, it is important to acknowledge that the requirements for success remain the same whether or not you agree with *how* someone chooses to be successful. Kim will never be able to live down her introduction to popular society and therefore may never be considered a credible or trustworthy individual by common standards. I can imagine how hard that must be to live with, knowing your work ethic and self-evolution will never be considered. In spite of all that, Kim continues to grow her network throughout the fashion and technology industries. She has been able to move through the commentary and locked doors to find the doors that will open for her and the people who are willing to give her a chance to prove herself. By definition, she has endured. And quite frankly, that is a major part of what it takes.

Oprah Winfrey, a media mogul, has had much to endure on her path to excellence as well. Though her path has been very different from Kim's, she, too, has had to endure criticism and obstacles as she sought to build her media empire. When Oprah made the decision to end the highly successful *Oprah Winfrey Show* to start the OWN Network, the media and her network peers went on the attack as she struggled to put together the right team. To embark on a new venture is hard enough without people commenting on your every step. Fortunately, Oprah had a network of people who could support her emotionally and professionally while she got her network off the ground. To me, this is an example of choice. When you are as successful as Oprah Winfrey, a billionaire, you still have to *choose* to be successful. The same way she chose to be successful as a local news anchor in Baltimore and face all the adversities that came with that position, she still has to make the choice every morning to get up and do the work. That is a valuable point to understand because success is a choice, regardless of what stage of excellence you are in.

My path has always been laden with my own unique set of adversities from abusive supervisors to dead-end career decisions and oppressive work environments. I have always struggled to find my employment fit. There is a delusion that I live by in which I believe I can actually find my fit one day. That is the idea that keeps me going from job to job in a trial-and-error process. I have suffered so much disrespect and downright ethical violation that I could write a book on that alone.

But I digress. My point is that you need to understand that the pursuit of excellence requires endurance regardless of your chosen profession: reality star, media maven, or corporate employee. Whatever it is you seek to achieve, you will have to endure something, and more than likely many things, before you actually achieve it. It is a choice to keep going. It is a choice to move beyond the criticism and hatred. Everyone has to find the doors that will open for them to apply their unique skills and abilities. No one is exempt from this endurance process no matter his or her stage of excellence.

For more than ten years, I have led teams to victory without the leadership title, salary, and comparable recognition. I have advised supervisors and leaders on how to perform their jobs. I have a history of demonstrating the competency and ability to perform at a high level within any environment, toxic or not. The excellence was always there but the lessons I needed to learn in order to achieve real success needed to take its time. That's the frustrating part about this. The only way through it is through it. And time likes to take its time.

You also have to learn how to endure the politics of the game because that's what this is: a game. A game of life, love, and prosperity. No one gets to achieve the dream without a cost to pay. As a young person, it becomes hard to know what's right in a world where wrong seems to win. For this, I like to rely on my spirit to guide me. I have turned down job offers and stepped away from potential suitors because my intuition told me so. You have to believe in your worth enough and trust that the right things will find you. Endure the path, find your patience, and allow what is meant for you to unfold.

Consistency

A man on a thousand mile walk has to forget his goal and say to himself every morning, "Today I'm going to cover twenty-five miles and then rest up and sleep.

—Leo Tolstoy

The race is not won by the swift. As I was a track-and-field sprinter from the time I was six years old, you can see how this took some time to unlearn. I naturally give intense, short-lived bursts of effort to my ideas and aspirations in hopes of obtaining a result. I never quite understood the value of stamina growing up. What I can say for sure is you have to develop and even increase your stamina as you move through the process of success. As you acquire more, you have to be able to give more to sustain what you have. You learn stamina through consistency; that is, consistent effort. Whatever it is you are trying to do—become a songwriter, climb a corporate ladder, lose weight, or start your own business—you have to give effort to what you want on a consistent basis. That means showing up every day to do the work. No shortcuts. This is not just to refine your craft or vision but to refine your skill and improve your stamina.

You will not always get the result you want every day, but you still have to show up. You may not always get the feedback that you want, but you still have to show up. It may take longer than you planned, but you still have to show up. You have to keep showing up even when you are discouraged, even when you've lost everything, even when there's no hope in sight, and even when everything about your circumstances says you're not going to make it and to give up. You still have to show up. Most people don't show up when it counts, but I would argue that people don't show up every day, and that's when it really counts. It's easier to be there when all you need to do is hit the winning shot at the end of game, but you'd better have practiced that shot every day in the gym outside team practice and on the weekends when it didn't matter if you want to get it right.

Will Smith, a movie and television actor, has had many successes over the years. He was once well known as a blockbuster king for the profitability of his summer films. When his films began to experience less success in theaters, his career came under fire. What I can appreciate about his journey is that the quality of his work hadn't necessarily declined. People may have changed their perception of him and his work, and the box office results may have been lower than those of his earlier projects, but he never became a lesser-quality artist in the way he approached his work. He remained consistent with his diligent work ethic. No one is in control of external variables such as public opinion and the outcome of his or her work, but you do control what you put into it. Despite the critiques, Smith still remained selective in his projects and showed up to give his best performance regardless of reviews, award nominations, or box office results. Consistency requires you to be steadfast in what you produce. You must remain disciplined and focused to move through the ups and downs of your path.

Jennifer Lopez, an all-around entertainer, has had an eclectic career spanning more than twenty years. Capitalizing on all her interests and talents, she has executed a formula for relevancy that is incomparable. With that, she has been very consistent in choosing projects that fit her skill set and delivering on every opportunity given to her. Even the constant narrative about her love life has never been able to deflect or derail her career progression. Again, her level of focus on execution and discipline to deliver have overshadowed any obstacles or commentary that followed her around. Half the battle seems to be just showing up.

In my own experiences, I have made it a point to tune out the negative antics and commentary as well. I have never known an experience that didn't result in some type of judgment about me as a person and a professional. As a young person entering the corporate world, I was often given the most impossible projects, toxic teams, and unreasonable standards. Regardless of what anyone said about me, my focus was always on results. That's one thing I knew: no one could deny it if I achieved. Despite the people who created roadblocks for me and the roadblocks themselves, I always managed to deliver eventually. It may not always have been a celebrated victory, and I may not have been the most liked person when all was said and done, but it was delivered, and to me, that's what counted: results.

Consistency is a hard concept to swallow because the

variables are always changing. People adjust their tactics to try to throw you off your game. Anomalies arise in the middle of progress forcing you to adapt and construct new solutions. Nothing in life really happens in a straight line. There are ups and downs, curves and sharp turns, and every other analogy you can think of to illustrate the imperfections of the process. You have to find your space of stillness and develop a commitment to your goal that is unwavering through every storm.

One of my bosses was a great example of how people explore tactics. She was a deeply insecure person who had a poor reputation and career history of underachievement. I assume this left her feeling a bit threatened by my work ethic, intelligence, and quality products. She started off with fear and intimidation tactics, as many of them do, to throw her title at me and threaten me into submission. When that didn't work, she tried to get to know me with a smile and sweet treats to see if she could persuade me to be compliant. She finally moved on to bullying and sabotage before she surrendered to understand that I was not her average employee. I knew my worth. I had a voice. And I was not easily broken. I wanted my work to be done right. I don't think there's anything wrong with that. But, when you are excellent at what you do and can drive results, it makes you undeniable, and no coward likes that. Be consistent in the effort and quality of what you do. They can never take that from you.

Resolve

Character cannot be developed in ease and quiet. Only through experience of trial and suffering can the soul be strengthened, vision cleared, ambition inspired, and success achieved.
—Helen Keller

People will test your resolve. That is a fact. It's like living in a shark tank where people try to get close enough to nip at you. Some want to suck on your goodness like algae eaters. Others take shots at your self-esteem and sanity like sharks trying to draw blood. People can be ruthless no matter how kind or meek their demeanor. They usually want something, which is why the company you keep becomes so important. You want to surround yourself with people who reinforce what you want to believe about yourself and your ideas, not people who tear you down at every moment of vulnerability. It is important to feel safe in your skin and in your own dream.

You must be totally committed to being who and what you are and do what you set out to do regardless of the many failures and distractions you experience. That is your resolve. That is what's being tested constantly through people, experiences, and inner demons. It is your commitment to what you want. It is your commitment to your potential, your unique expression of excellence. You have to develop a capacity for resiliency. You must be determined to recover, to get back up, and to keep going every time all the time.

Michelle Obama, the former first lady of the United States, described some of the adversities she and her family had to endure while in the White House. As a young African American woman myself, I was grateful to hear that I was not alone in enduring the disrespect, lack of support, barriers, and outright bullying that goes on when you are trying to deliver on your job and be successful. She mentioned how important it was to her experience that she had already had to navigate through hardships and develop a strong sense of self. She used her wisdom and resiliency skills to navigate through the nonsense not only for herself but also for her family. Though some may argue the success of the Obama administration, I believe she was successful in executing her goals of remaining whole as a person and keeping her family whole as well. She was so unwavering in her character under the spotlight that her actions were greater than any of the scathing remarks anyone could make. For this, she is my ultimate example of resolve, and I am incredibly grateful for the example she has left behind for humanity.

Rihanna, a popular music artist, has had her share of public humiliation. From an abusive relationship to naked photos to constant rumors, she is someone who has lived out a lot of things in the public eye. What I can appreciate about this individual is her resolve, especially for someone under the age of thirty. She may not be anyone's poster child for role modeling, but I invite you to consider what it must take to overcome some of her personal challenges and still create hit records. This is not an individual who gets taken down easily. There is a fierceness about her understanding of herself that makes her unapologetic, despite the judgments that people have about her and the adversities that she endures. Her "fuck you" vibe is actually quite appealing to many of her followers, and her resilience makes you enjoy her even more. Many people can live through horrific things, but not many can do it while the world is watching. That is someone with a strong sense of self.

I reflect on my own time in corporate atmospheres when I was called names, was told I would never be a leader, had individuals start rumors about me, and was even blamed for things I had nothing to do with. This was all done by people looking to position themselves for something they didn't think I deserved. I had earned my success every time, and every time I was denied my opportunity to excel. Someone less threatening, better politically positioned, and more appropriately complexioned was always more worthy of the appreciation, title, and pay I had worked so hard for. My character and kindness have been tested in every trial, and in every trial I choose to take the high road and treat these people with the dignity and respect that they take for granted, assuming privilege. To exercise resolve is a choice just as much as endurance or any other attribute mentioned in this book. And it is a constant rechoosing process every time you are confronted with adversity, assholes, or idiots.

One thing I've learned about resolve is how important it is to protect your health: mental, emotional, physical, and spiritual. It's more commercially acceptable to talk about physical and spiritual health than it is mental and emotional health. So let me be the contrarian that I can be and advocate for the mental and emotional. A strong mind is hard to break. Having awareness of your emotional triggers puts you in control of how you respond. As I've said before, people are going to try you, even if just for the sake of trying. You want to be mentally and emotionally prepared to handle such insanity and inhumanity. For this, you'll have to find your outlet. Whether you practice meditation, start weekly counseling sessions, or use the gym to sort out your grips, find something that keeps you focused and allows you to stay sane. I have had many experiences that have threatened to unhinge my mind and crumble my heart. A strong spirit will always seek to recover from trials and tribulations but I want you to consider not breaking or falling down at all. Find ways to develop your resolve.

Anchor

You always want to protect the thing that allows you to do what you do. Training is my anchor—it centers me and allows me to then work a full 12–14 [hour] day of business. Find your anchor. Protect your anchor.

—Dwayne Johnson

We all rely on something. Whether it's religion, spirituality, family, friends, a partner, alcohol, exercise, or therapy, we all rely on something to recenter ourselves and pull us through the hard times. Now I wouldn't advocate for alcoholism, but I want to be fair and illustrate that people anchor themselves and cope in different ways. It is important to study yourself to understand what will bring you back to center. Everyone gets off track and out of bounds sometimes. There are very few things in life that happen in a straight line. That being said, the goal is to create a sturdy foundation that allows you to come back to center and regroup.

Think of your anchor as your foundation. In order to build this sturdy house of prosperity, you need a strong, unwavering foundation to withstand the earthquakes, floods, and mob attacks that present themselves. It's not easy to build, and it definitely takes time. You have to know yourself and what you need to understand who should be around you. It takes time for people to reveal their true character and intent. You are bound to make mistakes when establishing your anchor.

Dwayne Johnson, a professional wrestler and actor, gave me the language for this concept when he described how he was able to manage his hectic work schedule at the height of his career. He called it his anchor. In an Instagram post, he narrated how he had driven hours just to go work out at one of his favorite gyms in the wee hours of the morning. Never mind the level of commitment and discipline that it takes to do something like that; I wanted to understand *why* he was doing that. As it turns out, that is how he refuels and recharges himself to keep going. Every person has to define that kind of process for him- or herself. Whether you are a teacher at the start of a new school year or a mom on her way home from work, you have to find a way to recenter, regroup, and recharge.

Tim Tebow, a professional baseball and football player, is probably best known for his commitment to his faith. After winning the Heisman trophy, he went on to have an arguably unsuccessful NFL career. He was the source of great controversy, considering how much hype had been given to his NFL venture. The public shaming and humiliation could have broken anyone, but he often credits his faith for pulling him through the disappointment. He explored other talents, which led to a professional baseball career, creating prosperity after a very public failure. His anchor of faith pulled him through that disappointment and allowed him to recenter on who he really was and what he was really worth.

I discovered after several near breakdowns that my anchor is solitude. I am naturally an introverted person, which means I recharge by being alone, not by surrounding myself with people. In addition, I am highly empathic, which means people tend to drain my energy anyway. In my early twenties, I started to withdraw from everyone. I am a person who runs at full pace, so it's easy for me to run myself into the ground, and trust me, no one will stop you from doing so. People will take, take, and take what they can get and leave you on the side of the road for the vultures to pick at.

Once I understood this viciousness, I began to work on myself and to discover my needs because I had to keep going. I was the only one I knew who was going to help me and make me successful. The universe responded to this intention and gave me allies to cross paths with who would invite me to different events or crack a door open in their professional networks. This gave me the opportunity to keep going, but I was going to have to find my fuel source.

Enter the rejuvenation of solitude. I started to pace myself when accepting invitations to events. I kept to myself during the holidays. Whenever I could feel myself getting run down, I would give myself a little people break to refuel. Everybody's anchor may be different, whether faith based, activity driven, or neither, but it is important to identify what helps you keep going.

I have watched many of my coworkers go on leave of absence in order to refuel. I never knew anything about that policy until I worked for a particularly toxic company. It was the most dysfunctional leadership team I had ever seen and they drove all of their talent crazy and put them out of work, doctor's orders. It was insane. I myself started to develop physical ailments out of nowhere. I was a fairly healthy young person who worked out regularly but I the stressors began to manifest physical issues. I was too young to understand what was happening. However, as I look back on that experience and continue to live through much worse, I am always reminded of what the process and people can do to you if you don't establish an anchor.

Network

The key is to keep company only with people who uplift you, whose presence calls forth your best.

—Epictetus

Nobody is successful alone. There are people who influence you. There are people who have gone before you who cracked open the door. There are people who invite you into the room. And there are people who give you an opportunity. Having a network of supporters, cheerleaders, and button-pushers has an important influence on your progression through the process. You also want to consider surrounding yourself with people who hold different perspectives than you do or those who are strong in areas in which you are weak to strengthen yourself. Always remain open to understanding the world differently. You want to continue to challenge yourself, and you want your perspective to continue to evolve. The company you keep can do that for you. If you are the "best" person in your friend group, you need new friends.

Now, it is important to understand the different characters you may find in your network. I wouldn't go so far as judge them as "good" or "bad" people, but you do need to understand what kind of effect these people can have on you and your process. If they can't elevate you or contribute something positive to your journey, then you might want to manage your time and energy with better care.

Two types I will call out are the "harmers" and the "hinderers." One intends to affect you negatively; the other does not. What's important is that both do affect you negatively. A harmer is a person who secretly wants you to fail and will advise you to take actions that will derail your progress. This is sometimes hard to detect because the advice may come from someone you trust or respect, and it is framed as advice. It is important to reflect on people's motives—not in a paranoid way, but understand that most people have an agenda, and it is not always to see you shine. I have experienced this with family members, people I called friends, coworkers, supervisors, and lovers. Anyone is capable of playing this role. I was enrolled in a professional development program that was designed to provide exposure and offer potential career advancement opportunities. That was the promise. For a few of the participants, their careers did advance. For several others, they quickly discovered it was all a hoax, just another way to get intel on employees. The program had strategic placement of buddies and mentors with departmental endorsement which gave their organization and supervisors the opportunity to keep a watchful eye on their talent and their talent's interests. I was well aware of my supervisor's controlling and paranoid nature so the fact that the program was run by her bestie, the buddy I was assigned was her other bestie, and the mentor I was assigned was the bestie of her boss, the chess game in play became quite visible. I was uncomfortable with the check-ins and mandatory coaching conversations because I knew no space was really safe for me to speak. Each coach said it was safe to talk. Each advisor offered just enough poor directives. And each seminar and conversation had my instincts screaming at me. As I used to tell my peers when they asked for my advice, you either use the program or the program will use you. In a matured decision, I decided to keep moving through the program to test my resolve and endurance. I was aware I was being tested. I was enclosed by harmers. I was going to have to create my own network to protect my career and build the opportunity to thrive.

A hinderer is a person who drains your energy, not necessarily with a malicious intent but definitely selfishly. I met a young girl who was eager to be my friend and kept asking me to hang out with her. I am always leery when people are too excited to know me. We finally had a few lunches together, and as it turned out, she wanted something from me. She always had a problem that needed resolve and wanted my sympathy and advice. This is not a friendship. This is a counseling relationship. You have to pay people for those kind of services. She was hindering me by draining me of my time and energy. I had to stop that. I had enough fake friendships where the person would want my company to be uplifted and encouraged only to abandon me when their life was going right. These people were never my friends. They were my clients. I had to be more mindful of that going forward.

Both of these types of people are equally harmful to the process. Their company must be entertained sparingly. They tend to soak up all your time, emotional support, resources, and wisdom, yet have nothing with which to reciprocate. By the time you've finished serving their needs, they are nowhere to be found.

Beyoncé Knowles, an iconic music entertainer, is notorious for her sense of privacy and guarded company. She is fiercely selective of the company she keeps and even more calculated in the interviews she gives. Beyond protecting her image/brand, I believe this caution is exercised for self-preservation as well. When you have the amount of pressure that comes from being both a global superstar and a brand, you need to preserve your sense of self to allow you to execute nearly flawlessly. For that, her family and her team of meticulously screened professionals support her in that quest for flawless execution and self-preservation. I can't knock her for that. I suggest you take care of your company as though your net worth were in the neighborhood of half a billion dollars, and you might see some adjustment to your prosperity, too.

Kevin Hart, a successful comedian, was a student of this philosophy as well. He spent time in the company of two professional writers and built relationships with as many mentors as he could to create the team of advisors that would help him reach the level of success he desired. Not everyone is born with a team of supportive people, and not everyone will have the support of people along their path. Sometimes you are required to manufacture it. No one will carry you, but most people are willing to give advice, considering it doesn't cost them anything but time and energy. Kevin seemed to understand this when consulting Chris Rock and Steve Harvey, two successful comedians who had come before him. He is one of the most shameless and unapologetic individuals I have seen when it comes to self-promotion and pursuing his own excellence. Knowing who can guide you toward your goals is a part of the process.

As an introvert by nature, I like to keep my network small. I've never needed an entourage to prove a point. However, you will always have many acquaintances who come in and out of your life. You still have to mind your company and protect your network. I am a person who likes to be inspired. For that, it is important for me to keep the company of those who can challenge me or teach me something.

For many years, I couldn't find that in my peers or friends. It was depressing. I was always able to give advice and inspire others, but no one added any enrichment to my life or story. I have had points in my life at which I'd fall into a valley of adversities, and no one had any empathy or encouraging words to pull me up. They just stood there and watched or worse, didn't even answer the phone. That hurt me for a long time, and I started to clean out my friend closet. I was tired of being of service to others but not having anyone there when I was in need. When people got their happiness and their men, they no longer knew my name. My company had to change.

I started forcing myself into my mentors' circles. This was hard for me as an introvert, but I was tired of the like-minded discussions. I needed answers to age-old questions. I needed a pool of people who could help me be a better person, be the person I wanted to be. I needed a new network, and that meant going beyond the people I simply met along my path. I had to look for them in the very places I wanted to be. When I look at the people I admire, they all have great teams. Each of them has a team of people who help him or her execute his or her excellence. Everyone on their teams has to rise to the same standard of excellence. Everyone has to show up and be great to look great. They make one another better. They have networks of excellence.

This means you have to associate with people who are, dare I say, greater than you, more accomplished than you, and so on. It's OK not to be the smartest person in the room. When you are in the process of striving, trust me, you don't want that. You want to fellowship with people who bring out the best in you. If you feel anxiety or anguish after visiting with someone, you might want to limit your contact with that stressor. People will absolutely be offended, but they'll get over it. If not, just think of how much pain and drain they've caused you and calculate whether or not you have the energy to maintain someone like that in your life while pursuing your excellence. Think of what you want to be carrying with you as you proceed through that journey. All I can say is, "Pack light."

Chapter 3
The Attributes

Self-Acceptance

I don't know if I continue, even today, always liking myself. But what I learned to do many years ago was to forgive myself. If we all hold on to the mistake, we can't see what we're capable of being. If we don't have [forgiveness] we never grow, we never learn, and sure as hell we should never teach.

—Maya Angelou

Throughout my work with individuals, I have found it fascinating how unaccepting we are of ourselves, never mind the insistent evaluation from others. We fail to give ourselves the love and approval that we need and instead crave it from those around us. Unfortunately and fortunately, their judgment cannot patch up the holes of despair inside us. Self-acceptance must come from within, and it is one of the most important things that we can learn to do. We need to forgive ourselves not just for the imperfections in our personalities but also for the flaws in our journeys. Despite the outcome, everything we've been through has gotten us to who we are at this point. Sure, in hindsight, there was always a different way to approach a situation, but we did the best with what we knew at the time. Still we won't forgive ourselves. We'd rather shame ourselves with our stories, hoping those around us can somehow heal the wounds with their approval. But what if they don't? What if your surroundings only reinforce your shame story and make you feel a sense of unworthiness?

Self-acceptance is an act of self-love. It's the thing I've had to work hardest to give myself because I could not find love and acceptance in my surroundings. One of the hardest things to do sometimes is to accept your own personality. You may not ever be accepted for who you are by the world, but you must, at a minimum, be willing to accept yourself. Most of us have experienced rejection of who we are at one time or another. Some of us have grown up being rejected every day of our lives by our parents and extended families. It is unfortunate if you add up all that constant rejection and use it to calculate your self-worth and value to the world. That score will always be low because everyone has his or her opinion of who and how a person should be, and not one of those opinions is any more accurate than the others.

Christina Aguilera, a pop vocalist, offered an example of self-acceptance to me, maybe to the extreme. During her *Stripped* album days, she gained a reputation of being "a bitch" due to her outspoken and strong personality. She grew so annoyed with the comments and characterizations that she just took ownership of the title. She started referring to herself as a bitch and miming behaviors that could be interpreted as bitchy but with a kind of sarcastic tone. While I don't necessarily agree with her choice to become what they called her, I do understand how you can get to a place where you accept that you're not a sweet, quiet country girl. Instead, you are a grown woman with an opinion. That has historically been threatening for many people. Instead of crumbling under the narrative, she decided to stand within it because she had a stronger sense of who she was than the people talking about her. For this, I admire her. Self-acceptance is not about you and other people coming to a consensus about who you are. Instead, if there is a real fact about you, you have to reckon with it, especially if it's not a quality you want to change. She knew she was always going to be a woman with an opinion. So she said if that made her a bitch, so be it. Done and done.

Drake, a rap artist, is another example of self-acceptance to me, this time to the other extreme. The early stages of his career were plagued with accusations of his being "too sensitive" and "emotional." As a male and a rap artist, you can see how this characterization could be a career killer.

What I love about his example is that he took a quality about himself that was mocked and used it in developing a successful career. He made a few well-reviewed appearances on *Saturday Night Live*, poking fun at himself and his emotions. He started making even more emotional mood music to market to the women who were responding to his feelings. I love that he used what was true about himself to his advantage. Some things about yourself you cannot change because they are a part of the person you are. Everyone is bound to have an opinion about that, but no one has the right to decide for you who you want to be. That is your decision.

Drake decided he liked being emotional and sensitive. That contributed to the creativity of his music. So he kept that quality and characterization and turned it into money made.

I have spent most of my thirty years on this planet battling for self-acceptance. I grew up feeling unloved and never good enough for my parents and family. I was often isolated and socially rejected by my peers in school, in athletics, and at work. I knew I wasn't like most people, but I didn't think that made me a bad person. I suffered through bullying, ridicule, judgment, and labels like every other human being. Despite my efforts to take the high road and deliver excellence, I seemed to always have a negative narrative following me around. I was "fat," "intense," "arrogant," "too emotional," "too sensitive," a "perfectionist," and "too driven." I was always somebody's problem and punching bag. But I'm not playing the victim here. I learned to take ownership of this unsolicited feedback and interpretation. I am thick with a womanly shape. But I was called fat at size four and size ten, so you tell me what difference it really makes. I am intense in that I am a passionate person. That doesn't work for some people. I am not arrogant, but I am confident, which is perceived as a negative quality to some people, especially because I'm a woman. I am emotional. It allows me to connect and feel empathy for others. I am sensitive. It allows me to tap into deep levels of my gifts. I am a perfectionist in that I care about the quality of my work. I am driven. I want something out of my life. I have a purpose. I like to give my best and do a good job. My brand is excellence, for Christ's sake! You can see how I decided to turn who I am into a business. After my twenties, I could see that there were certain parts of me that weren't changing no matter how hard I wanted to be different so people would leave me alone. Well, people still don't leave me alone. There will always be feedback that you have to endure about yourself. But I will say, I am happier just being who I really am knowing that it won't work for everybody.

Many of us have been conditioned to please, especially women and minorities. Being a young minority woman means that I am not acceptable to everyone, including society. I was born at a disadvantage, but like any disadvantaged person, I can use my journey to breed prosperity. I would argue that self-acceptance is a part of the resiliency process. You have to take an honest look at who you are and your circumstances and make choices from there. Release any shame or judgment and develop a willingness to see the advantageous side of being the way that you are. Most of your perceived weaknesses will be your greatest strengths. This is not an overnight process, but it is doable. You'll probably try many things before you get to the center of your truest self. Be kind and compassionate with yourself throughout this journey because it is just that, a journey. Besides, you'll have enough haters and commentators who will enthusiastically play their roles.

How To

After decades of feeling punished for who I am and how I look, I finally learned to embrace myself by owning my truth. That is, every time a boss criticized me for being too focused or serious (at work!), I'd say to myself, "You are absolutely right. I am very focused on driving results and these failing metrics are not making me want to laugh." I owned it. I care about my work. That's what I get paid to do.

When I'd come around my family and they would start judging or ridiculing me about my shape, exercise, or diet, I'd say to myself, "You're right. I do have a womanly shape, and I do enjoy food. I have curves, and there are people who like that." I also explored mirror work, in which I would name an imperfection and then say "I accept myself." I gravitated toward affirmation work via a recording, in which I read from a list of things I wanted to accept about myself and allowed the recording to lull me to sleep and penetrate my subconscious mind. You can get as creative as you need to inspire self-love. Remember, if you don't learn to love every part of yourself, it is most certain that nobody else will.

People cannot harm you when you accept the very thing they'd like you to reject. Do I emotionally eat? Sometimes. Do I distance myself from negativity?

Absolutely. Am I sensitive? Sure. Am I passionate? Yes. Can I be solitary? Of course. Take away their power by taking yours back. These people do not hold authority over your self-worth, so don't give them power over your self-esteem. They are looking for someone to project on, but it doesn't have to be you.

Try this exercise for yourself. Write down every complaint or comment someone has ever made about you that triggered a reaction or hurt you in some way. At the top of the page, write "I accept myself." Every time you read the list, look back at the top of the page and say, "I accept myself." It can be so freeing to accept who you are and all your perceived imperfections. Perfection is in the eye of the beholder, because just as there are people who can't stand that particular quality about you, there will be an army of people who adore it.

Focus

You will never reach your destination if you stop and throw stones at every dog that barks.
—Winston Churchill

I spoke earlier about the feedback of others. Now I want to make it clear that all that unrelenting feedback can turn into obstructive noise. Imagine a jackhammer demolishing a concrete sidewalk at six in the morning outside your home. Are you not irritated to pure rage by that sound? If you're not, congratulations: you have found inner peace. But for the rest of us, we need to learn how to focus on our intentions. When the crowd starts booing, this is when you get to test your ability to focus on what you came for. I don't use the word *test* to make you nervous but rather to alert you to the reality that this is an active process.

Let me familiarize you with the different types of noise. There are macroaggressive sounds like the abrasive jackhammer outside your home. There are microaggressive sounds like the stinging, high-pitched squeal of a scrape against the chalkboard ringing in your eardrum just long enough to make you crazy. I've experienced my fair share of both, but I will say the microaggressive experiences have been worse because they are a gentle wear and tear on you every single day. Before you know it, you are completely exhausted and angry without a clear idea of why.

A manager called me into his office for help one day and then proceeded to berate me for how I walked into his office, how I sat in his chair, how I talked, how I helped him, whether the help was timely enough, whether I was worth a gosh darn, and so on and so on. You can imagine I was more puzzled than moved by his antics. This was clearly not about me. He was looking for a victim to vent his woes on, and I was the ten o'clock meeting. Go figure. I couldn't take it personally, because it was an abrasive act that had nothing to do with any kind of cause and effect as a result of my presence. This person was clearly unhappy, and his unhappiness had nothing to do with me. This was a macroaggressive attack: an unjustified, abrasive attack without any provocation.

Macroaggressive attacks can also come from groups. During my track and field days, I had gone undefeated for a few years within my region. As an eleven-year-old, I recall a moment when I had finished a race and stood on the podium to accept my award. Without hesitation, a few crowd members, mainly parents, began booing me and shouting statements like, "Why don't you let somebody else's kid win? Do you think you're better than everybody?" As a kid, this floored me. First of all, I thought adults were supposed to be nice and supportive of kids. But more importantly, where was all this aggression coming from? I had simply run my race like everybody else had. I had trained for hours to produce a winning result. What was the problem?

The noise blared in my head as I stepped down and hid under the bleachers. I began to cry deeply, not understanding why I was being rejected for my excellence. Then I wiped my face and got prepared for my next race, but I couldn't stop crying. I ran around the entire track sobbing, yet I still won the race. I was so hurt, but all anybody else could think of was "Did she just win that race while she was crying?" Maybe it was focus, maybe it was the hours of training that pulled me through. Regardless, at some point during my warm-up, I had to decide to run my race. I had to focus on my intention of winning and go out there and do just that.

Being rooted against isn't a fun feeling, but it happens. I am not responsible for those parents feeling like their children weren't successful. This level of focus would later serve me well against more abrasive office antics. However, the constant nagging, complaining, nit-picking, and pettiness of my coworkers has always worn on my nerves. It can be easier to depersonalize a grand, abrasive act than to endure daily attacks on your work and disposition.

The office space is a deadly playground for microaggressors. I don't care how meek or friendly someone's demeanor may be, everyone has the capacity for this. I recently worked with a group of "subject-matter experts" who had a supervisor who enjoyed making degrading and demeaning comments about my work and abilities. Unfortunately, she set the tone for the team on how they would receive and interact with me. She would privately discourage my ideas and then claim them as her own in front of leadership for the credit. She made frequent put-downs during our one-on-one check-ins, such as "Because you're from corporate, you don't understand how to be a part of a community environment"; "Because you don't have a background in [this or that], you wouldn't understand what I'm talking about"; and "You couldn't do any of your work if it weren't for me and [your coworkers] because you don't have that kind of knowledge, and we wouldn't want that quality in your successor." Now this may not sound like much taken in small doses, but if you think about having a one-on-one meeting every week with a person who reminds you that he or she doesn't think you are good enough and takes great pride in finding fault within your work, this can wear on you after a while. These were microaggressive attacks on my self-esteem: cleverly disguised attacks masked as random and indirect comments. Subtle but deadly.

Coworkers are no different. My worth ethic always pushes the envelope in any environment, but I had recently joined an environment in which people were used to phoning it in. They would make snappy remarks to try to get a rise out of me. They would pretend to not see my e-mail requests so they wouldn't have to follow through on their work or act too busy to get something done then giggle as I walked away. They even went so far as to going to leadership to accuse me of hacking the company server when it went down because I was "the only one smart enough to do something like that." What the fuck? As a woman of color, I've been taught to keep my face and remain gracious in spite of any oppression. But I am human. In order to avoid the angry black woman stereotype, I have to put my head down and keep going. Standing up for yourself is important, but you have to learn to be calculated and pick and choose your battles. Developing the capacity to focus becomes critical in these instances. Celebrities are familiar with this kind of treatment as well, which is why it's important not to glorify their lifestyles. Whether it comes in the form of cyber trolls, bullying media outlets, or disgruntled industry peers, they are flooded with macro- and microaggressive activity all the time. Some accept it as a cultural norm as though it comes with the celebrity territory, but again, we are all human.

Jay Z, a popular rap artist and business mogul, took on the venture of sports management. He was asked about being investigated by the league for his involvement with athletes. He calmly replied that he wasn't fazed by the league's actions. He explained that he understood why the player's agents would be upset with his efforts. For years, they had been able to come to work and get a paycheck with little to no effort. Now that he was making an effort to actually help these athletes, they had to show up and do their jobs. The investigation was such an over-the-top response to his intention, he could hardly take it personally. It had nothing to do with him; it was about the agents' frustration with having to work a little harder than usual. They would have done this to anyone who made them show up and do their jobs. His intentions were clear, which made it easier for him to depersonalize the aggression and move forward along his path. Because the actions of the opposing party were so disproportionate to the circumstances, it made no sense for him to launch a counterattack. It was evident that these people were coming from a different space than where his intentions lay.

Focusing on your intentions can be much harder when you're facing a microaggressive action because it is unclear where the noise is coming from and whether or not you are causing it. It lingers in your ear at a distant decibel level just long enough to make you question your sanity. These are the pesky comments that people make that cause you to ask yourself, "Was that directed toward me?" Sneaky bastards. Furthermore, when you hear those comments every day, you can start to believe them if you're not careful. The weakening of the spirit can leave you vulnerable to absorbing their poison. After enough interactions like this, your self-esteem can wear away, eroding your happiness and self-worth one pint-size comment at a time. You'll find yourself adopting habits to cope with the anxiety caused by holding your anger in or trying to prove your critics wrong. Neither will address the insanity it causes.

Anna Wintour, a fashion journalist and editor of *Vogue*, has been characterized as a cold, harsh person. What a shame. I would guess this has something to do with her work behavior, regardless of whether it's true or false. Sometimes being a person of excellence creates misunderstandings of your intentions. An authoritative woman who knows what she wants can be a very threatening idea in this country, especially to other women. I like this example because the narrative surrounding who she is as a person has never disrupted the quality of her product. Allegedly, she was the inspiration for a character in a best-selling novel, *The Devil Wears Prada*. You can't feel more attacked or complimented than that. Her habits were captured in a successful book and a blockbuster movie. Though I don't suspect the book was written with any ill will, I can imagine the private feelings she must have felt about people judging her. At the end of the day, we are all human and reserve the right to be imperfect. To pursue excellence, you have to express extreme sides of yourself to move through conflict and accomplish something great. You might not be your best self every step of the way. That should be allowed. You're not shooting for an average product. Your goal in life should not be to be liked. I would hope you would aspire to more than that.

When people can't understand you or your success, they have to find fault or flaw to excuse themselves for not having the same. In this case, Jay Z doesn't know anything about sports management. Anna Wintour is mean to her assistants. What difference does that make? These people are trying to contribute to humanity by expressing their God-given talents. It is more than what most people will do in their lifetime of sitting on the couch, in the stands, or on the Internet commenting. Just like these excellent people need a break, so do you. If you want to be excellent, you have to release the idea that everyone will love you during every part of your journey. You will make mistakes and ruffle feathers along the way. Stay focused on your intentions and know that you seek to do good in this world by being exactly who you are.

We all get lost in the shuffle sometimes. The point is to notice it and get yourself back on track. The journey to actualizing your potential is long, so try to be loving to yourself when you feel like you've made a mistake. We are all learning and growing at our own pace. True greatness never fades. Dave Chappelle, a legendary comedian, left a hit television show and came back seven years later as a successful comedy performer. True excellence never dies. We can only hope that we are stronger and wiser about managing it our next time around.

I can't tell you how many bosses have admittedly tried to fuck me on my performance evaluations. One said it was customary for the rookie to take the L for the team. Someone had to score the lowest rating and though I had the highest sales, it made more sense for a rookie to be the underperformer. Another couldn't attack my metrics so she went after my character. She fabricated stories about how other people felt about me and how I handled situations to say I needed improvement. She submitted the evaluation without my knowledge and signature which caused Human Resources to reach out to me. When I confronted her about her statements, she said she was just angry because they were going to promote me over her. Obviously, none of this is fair play but you can see the issues going on within the attacker more so than anything else. You can't take it personal but it does suck.

How To

It's simple in theory but harder in practice when the noise has infiltrated your brain. I learned from a psychologist what it really means to be still. She explained that her culture had a proverb that said you are to be as peaceful as a tree in the thrust of a great thunderstorm. That image was powerful for me because that's what I felt like I was going through at that time in my life. A tree is very clear about what it is there to do. It is rooted in the ground. The leaves and branches may break off in the fray, but the tree remains steadfast and still.

If you're in the center of great conflict, ask yourself "What is trying to emerge in my life?" instead of fighting it. The fighting creates more tension. If you are being challenged on who you are or what to do, ask yourself, "What am I here to do?" Remind yourself of your short- and long-term vision. There will always be people, things, and ideas that try to distract you. If you truly want the long-term result, you've got to buckle down with a strategy to keep your attention and energy focused on the right things. People are going to do things that distract you from your purpose, whether it be in micro or macro form. It's never really personal. They'd attack anyone who was trying to live a better life than they had. Find a reason for compassion. When you get lost in the shuffle, it helps to find that space of quiet inside yourself. Evaluate what you control in the situation and release responsibility for the things you do not.

To focus, you have to mind the company you keep. Being in the workplace can be hard because we don't always choose our coworkers, but if you see that someone is a small-minded thinker, you are not obligated to engage with him or her beyond common pleasantries. Be mindful of entertaining empty rhetoric. Whether it's a destructive narrative about yourself or someone else, be mindful of how you use your energy. I know the warfare that can occur in your mind, but try to root yourself in the present moment. Find a space to wish people well, or don't, but let it go. Don't dwell. People have petty objectives. What they do is not your concern. I have been publicly shamed for bringing people doughnuts on Friday. You can't please unhappy people, nor is it your job to do so. Focus your time, energy, and attention on things that propel you toward the result that you want. This requires great discipline, but discipline can be practiced. Some days you'll have a victory; other days you will fall short. Keep going until it becomes a healthy habit.

Some people do this through meditation, going for a walk, working out, or listening to music—whatever works best for you. I used to write my intention on the whiteboard above my desk at work as a reminder. Then my strategy evolved into taking days off to break up my exposure to the nonsense. Some people take full-on leaves of absence to recover from abusive or emotionally draining experiences. There is no quick remedy for this. You'll have to play with it. Start to build a network of emotional support to help you purge those unproductive thoughts and theories about your situation. Having a supportive network can be priceless in combating the thought that you are alone in your struggle. That's what any of these villainous naysayers and emotional vampires would want you to think.

Blaming others for breaking your focus or knocking you off your intention is not going to help you actualize your excellence. Instead, expend your energy training yourself to be mentally and emotionally stronger. Train yourself to go beyond that little voice inside you that tells you it's OK to quit twenty minutes into your workout. Train yourself to be compassionate toward yourself after making mistakes. Train yourself so that as you pursue your potential, it is harder for you to be broken. You are allowed to be human, but to be great, you must learn to focus.

The ego can serve as a distractor, too. Though I see value in having an ego, you have to take care in how you use it. It can propel you through adverse situations by reminding you of how great you are, or it can derail your focus and energy by pursuing things that really don't move you toward your goal. For me, that goal is my desire for graduate-level education. My long-term vision is to get to a financial place where I can be my own boss, but do you need a graduate degree for that? Like many of my generation, I am tired of these old-school work paradigms that no longer work with our present-day societal structure. I am tired of the horrible bosses with no advancement opportunities and stale workflow. I want to be free to live my purpose and express my gifts. That's how you contribute to society and move humanity forward.

All my mentors have said I need a graduate degree in order to be taken seriously and excel. I don't disagree that this is a recruitment and promotion requirement by current standards. However, as much as I want to acquire a degree as a source of validation, it would be more of a personal accomplishment for me at this point, which makes it not as urgent. Let me be clear that it is one thing to want to accomplish something but another thing to think that it can validate you. Most of my friends have doctorate and master's degrees, and they're not doing any better pay-, title-, or experience-wise than I am. "So, what is the real advantage?" I ask myself.

At this point in my life, I found it more important for me to publish my first book to launch my own coaching business. That would move me further in the direction of being my own boss than a graduate degree would. For a long time, I wanted to pursue graduate school because I was insecure about my ability to teach the science of what know and afraid I was missing some critical piece that graduate school would provide. But what I know now is that the wisdom is already within me. The validation is in my journey, and the evidence is in how I've moved through every stage of it with traces of proven excellence in tow. I know many companies will disqualify me for not having a graduate-level education, but I am certain that I can do the job better than most people with or without a degree because of everything I've gone through. I'm not saying you shouldn't go to graduate school because that very well may be the appropriate thing for you to do. However, do it for the right reason—which I hope is because you really intend to *learn* something.

In my case, graduate school would have been a distraction from my long-term goals. At that period in my life, I would have been putting my energy into something that I wasn't ready for and that didn't advance my objectives. I had to refocus, and being clear about why you're doing something helps you do that. What I'd like to remind you is that everything will come in its due and right time. Focus on delivering in the present with what you have and what you have been called to do and deliver well on that. Success takes time—long hours without the spotlights of fame, praise, or prosperity. Nobody cares how hard you work, but you have to care enough to work hard. The salary will come. The leadership title will come. The acknowledgment will come. The academic achievement will come. Not all of it has to happen right now, but trying to make it happen when it's not your time distracts from what you really need to be doing and gives you an excuse to never do it. As long as you are veering off onto every side road, you don't have to be responsible for walking your path.

These particular distractions are born out of the ego. I believe I deserve to be paid a salary comparable to those of my peers, given the excellence I demonstrate in my work. I deserve to have a title that reflects my position as a leader of my team and organization and the direction and mobilization I create in those around me. I deserve to have a degree that says I am highly intelligent in what I do because I am exercising talents and gifts that are unmatched by the average person. I deserve, I deserve, I deserve. It's so easy to get stuck in what you deserve. This is why the ability to remain focused on the end goal is a skill you must develop over time and maturity.

Courage

I learned that courage was not the absence of fear, but the triumph over it. The brave man is not he who does not feel afraid, but he who conquers that fear.

—Nelson Mandela

Fear is an important topic to me because it is so prevalent in all our lives. It is a highly intelligent force that commands much of our attention. Fear can disguise itself as many different emotions and excuses. It can be an incredibly powerful tool or weapon, depending on how it is wielded. It's important to understand fear because its adversary, courage, is so desperately needed in order to become successful. As with any competitor, you want to understand your opponent, both its strengths and its weaknesses. This helps you defend yourself, if not defeat it.

We all struggle with fear. I do believe that in a lot of ways, fear is learned. When you watch a baby learn to walk, you'll notice the hesitation to let go of the couch, given his or her previous knowledge of what it feels like to fall. Whether the emotional pain of having failed at something he or she wanted so badly or the physical pain of hitting the ground, the fear even within a baby is real. As adults, the fear process is not quite the same. We still go through a bunch of cognitive evaluations assessing the risks and abilities involved in taking any leap of faith. Unfortunately, however, as adults we have acquired a lot more baggage that affects our ability to calculate properly. With years of hurt feelings and failed results, we've got much more to let go of than that little baby learning to walk for the first time.

Fear is a product of thoughts. Worrying about the future or being scared because of some pain from the past are common manifestations of fear. It evaluates the danger in any circumstance and assesses your ability based on past experiences and your current beliefs. From there, it talks to you about what you can and can't do. It is your choice whether you listen to it or not. The excuses you make about why you can't put yourself out there will not only delay your expression of excellence but can also completely derail it. Be compassionate with yourself, knowing that developing courage is a process. The only way to build the habit of courage is to practice it, in both large and small ways. Wherever you are in your journey, you have the right to be human. Some of us take a little longer to become masters at leaping off that cliff. Others leap right away, but as long as you eventually leap, that is the point.

Condoleezza Rice, former secretary of state for the George W. Bush administration, was quoted as saying that she couldn't wait for someone to be the first African American woman to hold the position of secretary of state because she was that woman. Or, as Barack Obama put it, the person you've been waiting for is you. You are the example of what you want to become. You are blessed if you can find mentors or supporters along the way, but ultimately, you are all you need.

Fear would have you believe otherwise, though. It can be disguised as laziness, self-doubt, chronic fatigue, procrastination, busyness, nosiness, and God knows anything else that you can conjure up to delay action. But like any competitor, it can be beaten. It has weaknesses, too. I've noticed that fear needs space and time to set in, so if you move before it can creep into your thoughts, then it cannot coexist with courageous action.

Ronda Rousey, a formerly undefeated UFC fighter, suffered devastating losses twice in a row. She was never known for her humility and had certainly made some outlandish remarks during her victory tour, but the chickens came home to roost on national television when she lost to a lesser-known fighter from the MMA world. I highlight this experience because of the courage it takes to get up from a loss. Then, to get up from a public loss. Then, to get up from a public loss after you talked so much crap about other people. I respect the humanity within this process. People will argue different things about her journey and how she handled it, but what is important to take away from this is that you will lose, and you will be required to get up from that loss and try again. I changed jobs many times before I found the right fit. Each time, it felt like a huge failure. That's the process of trying. You give your all, and you don't always get it right, but you try. That requires courage—acting in spite of your losses and fears.

I do believe that fear can be nurtured. Every time you have a painful experience and you fail to try again, your fear grows a little bit more to make you even more timid the next time. People can nurture fear within you as well. I come from highly fearful parenting. When parents are fearful, they tend to seek control by discouraging exploration within their child. I recall wanting to move to Los Angeles after graduating from college. You wouldn't believe the negative reaction I got from those closest to me at the time. One of my parents was afraid I'd end up being someone's street whore because I was so naive and inexperienced. A close friend thought I wasn't talented enough for the big city, and I'd end up a failure like everyone else and move back to Riverside where I belonged. A close family member thought the big city lifestyle was too fast for me and my sensitive nature, so I'd end up moving back in with my parents. I thought to myself, "Wow. Do these people even know me?" No, but they knew themselves. Every fear that lurked deep inside them was coming out at me for trying to be more than they thought I could be and certainly more than they were ever able to be.

Nonetheless, I moved to LA and suffered my share of disappointments, failures, and heartache, but I'm not a street whore, and I don't live with my parents. Though I had hiccups on the journey, I found myself more at home in a place where I had an opportunity to be seen than I was in a place where I knew I would not be. I needed to try. I was scared to death, but I had courage—the ability to act in spite of the fear I was feeling. I knew what I wanted, and I at least had to try to pursue it. Will Smith gave advice to an interviewer once, saying, "Find out what you want to do and do it without apology, or you'll never be happy." This rang true for me. I knew that if I stayed in Riverside I could make a life for myself, but I don't know if I would ever have been happy. I didn't want to turn into a bitter, timid dream killer like so many people I've known.

It took courage to obey the call. I packed up my things and moved to Los Angeles. I told myself I never wanted to be so afraid that I didn't move out of my comfort zone again. "I have to remain flexible," I would tell myself. Since there was no real example of anyone in my family who was anything I'd like to be, I had to trust myself every time I made a move. This makes it challenging because not every move you make is going to be the right one.

I remember going to a ropes course with an organization from my high school. The challenge was to jump off a one-hundred-foot tree. Everyone quickly sat down on a nearby log while a few adventurous spirits jumped at the opportunity. I fell somewhere in the middle, standing by my lonesome evaluating whether or not I should participate. I didn't want to be a fearful person sitting on a bench watching others live life, but I wasn't an adrenaline junkie either. I didn't want the fear to start talking to me, so I began to climb the tree. About halfway up, my hands started to tremble. Fear was setting in as I became aware of how far up I had come. I was breathing heavily as my body started to become fatigued. The assistance markers were fewer near the top of the tree. I was out of breath and trembling, standing over the edge. The only way down now was to jump. That voice started to have a conversation with me, so I leaped in midsentence. My feet landed on the ground. I was OK, and I had lived.

How To

Nobody is brave all the time, so let's not set an unrealistic goal. I want you to learn how to be brave most of the time. That means every time you have an opportunity to practice courage, do it. I used to make myself go skydiving, zip lining, rock climbing, anything that would provoke my inner fears just so I could confront them. I wanted to get good at feeling fear and then going beyond it. Practice makes perfect, and every time you win, you get a little more confident. The objective is to grow to where your courage becomes much more powerful than your fear. Whatever you think you can't do, just do it. If you fail at first, find out what didn't work and do it again. Don't allow the fear to have space and time to think too much. That's how it paralyzes you into inaction. You may want to explore an exercise in which you write down your fears and then take action to face them. Both small and large fears count. Living courageously is a process of constant rechoosing. Every day that you wake, express a willingness to walk with more courage.

Confidence

Man often becomes what he believes himself to be. If I keep on saying to myself that I cannot do a certain thing, it is possible that I may end up really becoming incapable of doing it.
—Mahatma Gandhi

Self-confidence is a powerful tool for becoming successful. How many successful people have you seen who barely have any talent? They believe in themselves so much that others learn to believe in them, too. Think about it: you've got to believe in your own product; otherwise, it will be hard to sell it. I also find that these people show up for their opportunities. They don't waste a whole lot of time worrying about perfection because they know their confidence will overshadow the quality of their product. They do what they know how to do and focus on doing that well.

Kanye West, a rap and fashion artist, is someone who has taken this advice to the extreme. As talented as he is, he is better known for his ego and his rants. I recall hearing his story of rejection, in which he made a conscious effort to think highly of himself to overcome the rejection he experienced from the music industry. He figured that if he could believe in himself intensely enough, others would eventually follow suit. People not only began to believe in him as an artist but they came to crave his rants. In this example, confidence fueled his creativity. It gave him freedom to explore the boundaries of what he could do without the apprehension of failure.

Chris Brown, a pop and R&B artist, has had his share of adversities and bad press, too. He takes ownership of his infamousness with his Instagram tag line as "the one you love to hate." His demeanor can be quite hate-able at times: he is very cocky, but his talent is undeniable, so most people have come to respect him. He suffered one of the most embarrassing and character-killing experiences when his abusive behavior toward women became public knowledge. People literally wanted to end his music career. I would argue that his confidence not only pulled him through his bad stunts and behavior but also put him back in popular demand through the quality of his music. Sometimes you have to become a bigger version of yourself to overcome the great amount of adversity you are enduring. Most well-accomplished people have experienced very unnatural things. While I don't encourage his behavior, I understand it. To play the role of the villain can be harder than playing the role of the hero. To inspire people to open up to you even when they want to hate you is a pretty remarkable thing.

I have had my own experiences with extreme confidence at times. I was taught early on that failure was not an option for me. In college, I took a literature class with a professor who, unbeknownst to me, was well known for barely passing his students. On my first paper, I received a C. For a career A student, this was appalling. My roommate told me, "What did you think you were going to get? Nobody gets As in literature class. Nobody can do it. Just accept it and move on. You only need to pass anyway."

This was enough spark to light my flame of confidence. I went to every office hour in search of a professor who'd rarely show up. When I did manage to catch him, he was perplexed by my persistence. "Why do you care so much?" he asked me.

"Why wouldn't I?" I replied.

Amused, he began to share with me what he wanted to see in my writing style. I went back several times with new drafts to make sure they met his criteria. I got an A on that paper and in the class. My roommate looked at me in disbelief and annoyance. I wasn't worried. I knew who I was. I was excellence.

Self-confidence doesn't always have to be present at first in order for you to succeed. People grow into their confidence much like they grow into their courage: one act at a time. When I first started making my way into the leadership development field, I was intimidated by the seniority of the team I was working with. All of them had been leadership development professionals for years. I got the opportunity to facilitate my first class, and I was incredibly insecure about my abilities. I knew I was going to have to believe in the product I was selling in order for others to buy it. I studied, practiced, interviewed others, and practiced some more until the time came to perform. I felt so nauseous. I just knew the audience would see right through me and my inexperience.

When I walked into the class, I made a point of standing up straight and walking with my head high. My fingers were trembling as I readied the paperwork, something I hoped none of the managers could see. I decided to project my voice in a firm and clear tone to give the illusion of self-assurance. I wasn't ready, but I was going to act like I was. As soon as I spoke my first paragraph's worth of words, my voice tremble dissipated, and my inner "Sasha Fierce" emerged. I was animated, playful, and energetic, an entirely different person, as one of the attendees noted. She said, "You become someone else when you teach." I agreed. I was so surprised by the positive feedback and the comparisons to the most senior individual on the team. I had natural talent, but I didn't believe in it yet. I had to fake my way through it before it became true for me. At the next class, I was equally nervous but more aware of my strengths.

I haven't always been confident in everything I've done. I battle with self-doubt like everybody else. The difference is that fear greatly annoys me, and I don't enjoy being too afraid to do something. It has delayed me, but it never quite prevents me from jumping off a cliff. I guess I've learned to believe that I can bounce back, whether I'd like to or not. I do, however, have the fear of crumbling under too much negatively because I once crumbled as a child. I try to avoid negative people and situations, but as an adult, that is unrealistic. Instead, I have to believe in my own abilities to rise from every fall, to deflect every criticism, and to stand in every moment of conflict. I have always been a survivor. I want to become a thriver, and to thrive, you have to master your ability to survive.

Being your greater self can be painful and feel exhausting. There were many times in my life when I wanted to give up and go away. There were many more times when I've asked for it all to stop, to end, to be done already, but that wasn't the point of actualization for me. My spirit wasn't finished yet, so I had to keep going. I've tried to reduce myself to blend in, but I am not your ordinary person. I do not belong in average environments, and neither do you. When you try to betray who and what you are, your spirit will gleam until you acknowledge your essence. You cannot hide from yourself, nor should you be trying to hide yourself from others. It's OK to confident. It's OK to be secure. We are taught to be uncomfortable with owning our power and acknowledging our abilities. No one is telling you to walk around whipping people with your intelligence, but you do need to take ownership of what you bring to the table and do so unapologetically. No one is as great as you at what you do. No one.

Knowing what you bring to the table helps you move through the commentary because you know that what you do is undeniably great. Greatness isn't for everyone because not everyone is in a space in their lives to handle it. You are not responsible for anyone else's journey, only your own. When people are threatened by your confidence and demonstration of excellence, they can simply see the passivity of their lives through you. Even the greatest of talents have to grapple with their own confidence. Beyoncé famously created her alter ego persona "Sasha Fierce" to give her the confidence boost she needed to do some of the things she wasn't comfortable doing onstage. If you watch her documentaries, you can see her battles with fear and insecurity, trying to convince herself that she could wear that outfit or perform to that number of people. The point is not that she has fears and insecurities but that she goes beyond them, even if she has to step outside herself to do so. In this way, self-confidence is one of the qualities that can be manufactured. You can learn to believe in yourself by putting yourself out there over and over again. Whatever you are afraid of, do it and do it again. It's much like developing courage. You will grow in your belief in yourself every time.

We can all be broken and beaten by life's experiences, and we will need to redevelop ourselves into the people we once were. I used to be a champion in track and field. I experienced so much criticism and pain from my coaches, family, and peers that I minimize myself and abandoned the sport. I couldn't crawl out of that tunnel of shame I had gotten into. I believed I wasn't good enough, strong enough, gifted enough to withstand the journey. That loss of confidence haunted the subsequent years of my life. It took nearly twenty years to recover from those experiences, and I'm still not fully myself. I have to retrain myself to be that champion again because she is still in there somewhere. She is afraid, exhausted, and unsure, but she is present. She will never die.

How To

Where can you find self-confidence? Within yourself, of course. You can't go around looking for others to believe in you with this one. You've got to believe in yourself. All the compliments in the world won't fill up this empty cup. You've got to do it yourself, and it starts with courage. I have watched great talents fall when they failed to believe in themselves. Believing in yourself is crucial to the process of actualizing your potential. In order to thrive, you have to believe that you deserve to do so. You have to believe that it is a possible reality for you. It is something you must choose and rechoose, time and time again. Throughout my journey, I have had to choose and rechoose to be successful, excellent, courageous, and self-accepting. Even if at times I've been incredibly reluctant and resistant, I still make the choice to get back up and fight to pursue what I believe was born deep inside me. I wasn't born to be average. I wasn't born to be to be complacent. I wasn't born to fit in, and perhaps, I wasn't born to be liked. I was born to be great. Not fitting in is my best asset and my most cunning demon. Being confident in everything that you are is a perilous journey, but it can be done. It starts with the self. Then you put your product out there and give yourself a chance to thrive. This is what you were born to do.

If there is an area of your life in which you want to be confident, write it down and pursue little actions toward it every day. Nothing has to start off grandly. You want to build the perception that you can be successful, so start with little goals. You can also practice with affirmations, whether recording your own and listening to them on the drive to work or writing those positive beliefs down and committing them to memory. Do things that you know you are good at and compliment yourself afterward. It may feel silly at first, but it's OK to say that you're the shit at what you do. Remember, you've got to believe it in order to project it.

Resourcefulness

It's not the lack of resources, it's your lack of resourcefulness that stops you.
—Anthony Robbins

Being able to create your own opportunities, answer your own questions, and devise your own plan are real strengths. So many of us want to sit back and wait for someone to help us get to where we want to be, but nobody can be or should be more invested in your prosperity than you are. Besides, most people who actually can help us would rather help someone who chooses to help him- or herself. After all, nobody has time to carry others around. We've all got our own burdens to bear. Do yourself a favor and become resourceful.

I will admit there is a devastating lack of mentoring in our culture, and as millennials, we long for it. But news flash, my peers: nobody is coming to help us, so it's wise to figure out how we can help ourselves. I say this from experience, as someone who has voluntarily mentored others who were waiting for the world to tell them what to do next. Most people are willing to attach themselves to something that is already successful or a rising star. Be the rising star, and you will get the help you seek.

Think of Internet sensations like Justin Bieber, Michelle Phan, and Lilly Singh. Each of them built a following online before he or she landed mainstream acclaim. We are in a day and age when you can do that. You just have to be resourceful. I would argue that none of these individuals knew everything they needed to know about their craft in the beginning. They just got started, and their success began to snowball after a few years of hard, consistent work. You don't necessarily have to know people either. Marie Forleo, a life coach, has said that she didn't know any famous people when she got started doing her work. She didn't come from wealthy parents either. Instead, she had an interest and learned how to market herself online. That grew her following to the point that she can speak at OWN Network events and host her own television show. Not everyone will get to do those things, but the point is to invite you to be creative in how you build relationships and forge your path.

It is not as uncommon as you think to start from scratch. I, too, have stepped into many arenas where I didn't know anybody and had no prior navigational knowledge. In those instances, I would research people online or find an area of the business I was interested in and look up a contact. Sometimes people were friendly. Sometimes they weren't. I'd introduce myself to people I didn't know. Invited myself to different events. When you truly need something, that's when resourcefulness will outweigh your fears and insecurities. Remember, I'm an introvert, and I did all this networking activity.

I also think naming your intention helps. I am a spiritual person, so I believe in communicating with the Creator. I have learned just to say exactly what I want with clear intentions and then trust that it will present itself.

Somehow, a resource would cross my path that would lead to the thing I requested. You still have to be ready and open to receiving it, but it will eventually appear. For example, I was new to an organization, and I needed to make a contact outside my department to find someone who could help me get my job done. I didn't know anyone, and nobody on my team was willing to help. I became really determined not to fail. I set my intentions with God. As time went on, I kept running into this particular person in the elevator. I didn't know who she was, but we would exchange pleasantries. I still didn't have a resource, though. I decided to go online and research names of people in the department. I found a few who looked appealing, so I sent them an e-mail. Only one replied to tell me to contact someone else. I contacted that someone who directed me to another someone. I was getting closer but still had no resource. Finally, in another brief exchange, I found out that the person I needed to meet had been in the elevator with me all along. I now had a few names I could drop to build the credibility I needed and foster a relationship that would provide the help I was looking for. It worked like a charm. This person knew someone who knew someone else and that someone else knew someone else, but I'd followed through on every invitation until the job was done. I had all the resources I needed to go forward and got a few job propositions to boot. You can't be afraid to put yourself out there to ask stupid questions, make friends with strangers, and look up information yourself. You're not going to get it all right, and it's not going to work every time, but it will work.

How To

Develop friends where you need them. Think of what resource you need, and put yourself in the arena with those who have it. Find resources with the right information.

Not everybody's advice is warranted, so listen with a filter and compare opinions. Ask several people before you make your decision about who to believe. You want to gain insight on who to ask for what and when. Timing can be everything. When I first moved to LA, an actor told me a story about auditioning that stuck with me: be nice to everybody. You never know who knows who. Los Angeles is a big city but a compact place. You are bound to cross paths with someone who knows someone you need, so be kind. Become your own advocate, and others will want to advocate for you. When you demonstrate that you are a go-getter, most people want to get behind that. Brand yourself as someone people want to support. Believe in your dream so strongly that others want to believe in it, too. It is then that resources will find you.

Chapter 4
The Conditions

We are all in the gutter, but some of us are looking at the stars.
—Oscar Wilde

Let's be honest. Most of us did not grow up or even end up in the right conditions to be successful. It would be a disservice to focus on what makes someone a victim because everyone's situation is different. Research has tried to narrow down that criteria, but I'd rather not dwell on the specifics of one situation. As I've said before, I'm more concerned with how you move through it. We know that adversity breeds friction that can create maturity and wisdom. We know obstacles can establish character. We know resources are a contributing factor to fruitful opportunities. And we know timing plays a role in it as well. Instead of listing all of the possible scenarios that exist, I'll simply offer commentary on the matter and refocus the discussion on creating the conditions that produce success instead of worrying about all the variables that cannot be controlled.

I will go back to my reference of Carl Rogers as his research mapped out the criteria for self-actualization. In brief, it requires you to have your basic needs met before you can truly focus your energy on thriving (McLeod 2007). So basically, if you can't get a decent meal every night, you probably aren't going to be focusing your attention and resources on your dreams. The same applies to living check-to-check. If you are struggling to keep the lights on, you probably don't have much time to dwell on other aspirations in life. You've got to deal with your basic needs first. I would suspect this is why many people struggle to maintain their focus. There are not just genuine distractions in life but competing priorities. Once you have your basic needs intact, it's easier to think about what you want out of life.

By now, we've covered all the presumed requirements and established a definition of what it means to be successful. I'd like to revisit preparedness as a contributing factor to success. By fulfilling the requirements and developing the attributes of a successful person, one should be *prepared* to receive successful outcomes, right? In theory. Now this is the part of the book that will start to sound esoteric because there is an undefined divine element involved in it. I am not God, so I cannot say for sure how it all works, but there seems to be an element of "chosenness" to this thing called success, especially at certain levels. Now, that isn't to say that you cannot be excellent at what you do. You are on this earth, so you were chosen to be excellent at something. However, I don't think everybody is meant to be Beyoncé, and I don't think everyone will become Bill Gates.

Everyone can achieve personal excellence. You control whether you give your best to yourself, your life, and your work. You can be successful on your own terms. That is why it is important to be clear on how you define success, rather than how society defines it. Many of us will find ourselves chasing standards that are not meant for our gifts. There is a level of fame that will come with being excellent because excellence attracts attention in a world of mediocrity. However, not everyone will become famous from the expression of their gifts, and that's OK. It doesn't make your life or your gift any less valuable. Take a moment to digest that.

Now as for conditions, see your journey as the conditions. Everyone has a unique path and process to his or her own self-actualization. The attributes and requirements described here are simply the parallel patterns found in everyone's journey. The process, I believe, is hand-crafted by both you and God. It is what lessons are given to you and how you respond to those lessons that determine your capacity to grow into the person you need to be. I believe everyone has come to this earth to do something, to give something, and maybe even to teach something through his or her existence. How you move through your life circumstances is what influences the timing and the possibility of you achieving your own excellence. Everyone makes mistakes. Everyone experiences delays. Everyone has a level of hardheadedness. But ultimately, we do have a choice in whether or not we pursue and achieve our purpose.

I remember reading once that we choose our parents and family before we come to this earth. As spirits, we choose the conditions that will help us achieve the spiritual evolution we need while on this planet. That means we choose the loving and abusive childhood environments. We choose the poverty-stricken and wealthy upbringings. We choose the abandoning and supportive characters we call our families. We choose this beforehand to help us develop the resiliency and skills we need to express our gifts. Controversial thought, I know. And it sucks to think of it that way because who would choose such a dismal life for him- or herself? But think of it this way: you wouldn't be the wonderfulness that you are if you hadn't gone through such adversities. Because your parents were so unloving, you learned how to love. Because you grew up so broke, you learned how to make money. Because your family was so unkind, you learned how to take the high road. I'd like to believe it is all for a purpose.

The point is to use your conditions, whatever they are, to your advantage and create the life you want. I am not as concerned about how each condition limits you because we all have things that we have to work through. Instead, find the alchemy in what you've been given. I think of all the horrible things people have said and done to me over the years, and all of it has become the story that I use to enlighten and empower others to persevere and be excellent. That is the gift of alchemy that I have been given. Though adversities and unkindness certainly feel like a painful burden, I choose to use them to motivate me and even to fuel my creativity. Do not concern yourself so much with your conditions because they will change. Instead, consider how you can use them to create the life that you want.

Chapter 5
The Calling

Have the courage to follow your heart and intuition. They somehow already know what you truly want to become. Everything else is secondary.

—Steve Jobs

Following your intuition sounds simple enough, but with all the voices in and outside your head, it can be hard to see the forest through the trees, as my science teacher used to say. Think of how difficult it must be for your intuition to get through to you with all the barreling distractions around you. However, following your intuition is an important skill to develop. I call it a skill though I understand intuition is something that is innate to all our beings. The skill is learning to listen to it, allowing it to guide us. That must be learned and all our other bad habits unlearned.

One of the things I've noticed about successful people is that even with all the noise around them, they still choose to follow their intuition. Jennifer Lopez, a famous actress and performer, has spoken about her mother being against her getting into show business because she didn't understand her vision. But "Jenny from the Block" had a dream that she was supposed to be in show business. Despite the noise, she followed her intuition and pursued her opportunity to become what she is today, a full-blown brand. Justin Timberlake, a pop musician, had a similar encounter with the thought that it was time to leave his world-famous singing group. He had finished one of their biggest tours and had a strong feeling that it was time to move on. Who would want to move on from a world-famous boy band making tons of money traveling the world at the top of their game? Justin followed his intuition to move beyond logic and reason and launch his solo career. His decision proved to be a very successful one, in future years earning him the Michael Jackson Video Vanguard Award.

Intuition is difficult to listen to because of logic and reason. All the rules we've been taught and the boundaries we are not supposed to cross are designed to protect our safety. But they are not always relevant when pursuing the extraordinary. When you are looking over the ledge wanting to experience flight, the only way you can do that is if you jump. Well, logic and reason say that doesn't make much sense without a parachute because you're going to fall. Logic and reason are calculating the distance to the ground and assessing whether staying in your current position is a safer option. Which, in most cases, it is. These rules and boundaries keep us safe, but they don't necessarily allow us to thrive. They give us the predictable, steady life that we all can achieve to last us through our retirement years. Remember, pursuing the extraordinary can sometimes be perceived as a task that only the crazy or masochistic pursue. Will Smith mentioned that there is a certain level of delusion that is required to access your inner greatness. He referred to the example of the once-impossible concept of an airplane. Bending a piece of metal and flying that piece of metal over the ocean was once a crazy idea. But we fly in planes all the time now. Walking across the room and flipping a switch to make the light come on was once a delusional concept as well. You have to believe that you can make the impossible happen. Most people wouldn't understand why you would want to even try, let alone that you could actually do it.

I have had my encounters with radical judgment calls

at times. Whether it was overwhelming fear or my intuition, I knew something was calling me to move. When I enrolled in my counseling psychology PhD program, I was ecstatic at first. I thought I had my life figured out for the next six years. Within one quarter, things had taken a turn for the worse, driving me to leave the program. I consulted nearly everyone who would take a meeting with me to rationalize my feelings, but no one really agreed with me. I went through so much inner turmoil I nearly drove myself insane. My brain and my intuition were in great disagreement. How could I leave such an incredible opportunity? How could I walk away from my chance at graduate education? Didn't I realize how many mentors I was going to disappoint? Did this make me a failure now? The questions raced through me, but ultimately, I walked away. On paper, it seemed like a big mistake, but in my body, I felt something peaceful. Trust me, it sucks to watch everyone else around you get a graduate degree when you know you were on the path to do the same. But honestly, my gift hasn't changed. Not having a degree doesn't make me any less wise at what I do, regardless of those who may beg to differ.

The point is I had to listen to my intuition, which was screaming so loud it started to negatively affect my health and happiness. I went to a dark place and started to become mentally and physically unwell. A few years later, I went through the same thing at work for a corporation I had a lot of respect for. I moved to the middle of nowhere just to have the opportunity to work for this company. Again, I was quickly informed that this was going to be a bad deal. My supervisor went missing for the first three months. The team of employees I inherited were considered "departmental rejects." There was no guidance or resources provided by headquarters. I was alone and labeled an outsider. I was picked on, sabotaged, disrespected, and abandoned until I started to turn over results for the team. Suddenly, people wanted to participate in the success. Magically, the delinquents were no longer delinquents but quality employees. The struggle to cure a rotting environment and transform it into a functioning and productive workplace had taken its toll on me and my health, though. My intuition had told me it was time to leave long ago, but I was chasing a career opportunity I was never going to get. After the company played me out of a transfer opportunity and my health problems escalated, I finally left. No job, some savings, but free from a very toxic experience.

The mental and physical strain I was under every day combating macro- and microaggressions, the depressing isolation, the long commute, and the dead-end job all began to add up. It just wasn't worth it. My intuition may have been telling me all along, but I respected the opinion of the logic and reason more. In the end, I had to learn from it. That's all I was able to take with me. This pattern began to repeat itself again at my next job until I ran across an old college friend who was enduring similar conditions. Her patterns had led her through worse employment experiences in order for her to learn certain lessons. We admitted that we were very hardheaded people. As I listened to her exhaustion on the ride home from work, I started to wonder, "What part of us is contributing to these experiences?" The only commonality I could find had to do with our inability to follow our intuition. We kept searching for a different path, trying to avoid the one we were designed for. We would take on these impossible circumstances to prove our worthiness and then find ourselves disappointed and exhausted with no reward. We could have avoided all this agony and delay had we taken a deep breath and turned within to listen to the silence, the knowingness that was there all along.

It took my friend getting fired and me passing out from nausea-inducing migraines to stop and listen. Intuition is a gift, but it's a very tricky thing to understand when you are a young adult. You have so many of your own facts, figures, and calculations that it becomes hard to trust something intangible. Ultimately, no one will truly know what's right for you but you. You can talk to as many people as you want, go to therapy, consult an expert, but no one can make that decision for you. And ultimately, no one will experience the consequences but you. What both my friend and I had to learn from those experiences was that we can survive anything. If we can achieve extraordinary results for these companies with the worst people and the worst circumstances, we can create greatness for ourselves. That is true for you, too. Unfortunately, what can often stand in our way on the very path we seek is ourselves. You have to gain a trust and comfort level with being still. If you ask, be patient for an answer. If you want something specific, be willing to hold out for that specific thing. If you're unclear of what to do, then don't move. Allow your spirit to speak to you and through others to find what's right for you.

How To

People have different methods of achieving it. Meditation, prayer, quiet time, dreaming. There is no right way to hear your own spirit, but silencing the inner and outer noise is a key element. I have been able to hear it as a faint voice while the chatter in my head was screaming. I have seen signs in nature that affirm that I've made the right decision. I have even felt a presence and energy that let me know I was being guided. Intuition manifests itself in different ways for different people. There is no wrong way to receive the message. The key is to listen to it. I encourage you not to wait until something horrific or life changing alarms you.

In other cases, it's as simple as just asking the spirit what you want to know. Just ask the question and be quiet. You may not get an answer in the next five minutes or five days, but it will reveal itself. Be careful of preconceived answers, though. Sometimes you think you know the answer or want a particular answer so badly that you only want to hear and see things that confirm what you want rather than what's best for you. Life is not always about the short gain. I have passed over many opportunities that seemed more fruitful in immediate terms and later found out they blew up shortly after someone else took the offer. I have left opportunities prematurely because I was following my ego instead. Your intuition always has your best interest at heart.

Epilogue

Perfection is not attainable, but if we chase perfection we can catch excellence.

—Vince Lombardi

Everybody has the potential to be extraordinary, but each individual must choose that for him- or herself. Surprisingly, though, not everyone wants to live an extraordinary life. Let me clarify: most of us want to be associated with an extraordinary lifestyle because we think it's better than our own. However, few can stomach actually living it. Think of the dangerous pursuit of fame these days. Or the classic pursuit of riches. There is a lot that comes with all of it that goes unsaid. People don't get into the limelight by accident, and not everyone will be able to sustain the burning glare.

Most wealthy people rarely have the time to enjoy their wealth. Their big house by the marina, the fancy car they never drive, the vacations they never have time to take—all seem fantastic from the outside looking in. How can it be so unenjoyable? You have to work to maintain excellence. And sometimes that means working when others are sleeping. I can say for myself that I don't get a lot of sleep. Ideas keep me up at night because I want to make an impact in the morning. When you don't aspire to much, you don't have to ready yourself in the morning. You just wake up and do what you did yesterday.

I want to reemphasize that greatness is a choice, but we have all been chosen for something. I especially want to note that everyone's level of greatness will be different. You cannot aspire to someone else's excellence. What others have (and what others are going through) may not be appropriate for you and your spiritual evolution. I use the example of Beyoncé because so many of us fantasize about living her life. Not everyone is supposed to rise to that level. I used to say, "Not everybody is supposed to be Oprah." Your impact on the world will be unique and significant enough. You are meant to touch people in interesting ways just by being who you are and having your unique history.

You must learn to persevere through adversities in order to actualize your potential. Each challenge is not an attack on your well-being but an opportunity for you to meet yourself in a new way. You can choose to simply survive life if you want. You can choose to live safely and quietly if you'd like. You can choose whatever is going to make you feel happiness, which is what we are all in pursuit of. But please know that no matter what you have chosen for yourself, you were born to thrive.

Reference

McLeod, Saul. 2007. "Carl Rogers." Last modified 2014. *Simply Psychology*. http://www.simplypsychology.org/carl-rogers.html.

About the Author

Kamaria Heru is a development consultant for KA Coaching & Consulting Services. She has spent most of her career as a training and development professional for Fortune 500 corporations and has mentored students at the top universities. She coached undergraduate students and employees for nearly ten years before starting her own business and becoming a self-improvement author. Her work mainly addresses self-actualization by identifying the criteria for success and encouraging self-awareness. Her belief is that excellence is possible for everyone, but we all must choose that path for ourselves.

www.ingramcontent.com/pod-product-compliance
Lightning Source LLC
Chambersburg PA
CBHW060348050426
42449CB00011B/2876